PERFORMANCE ASSESSMENT TEACHER'S GUIDE

6

Cover and Title Page Photo Credit: ©imagewerks/Getty Images

Printed in the U.S.A.

ISBN 978-0-544-56942-3

5 6 7 8 9 10   0928   22 21 20 19 18 17 16

4500614451   A B C D E F G

Approaching Performance Assessments with Confidence

By Carol Jago

The best assessments reflect best practice. Rather than asking students to perform artificial tasks, assessments worth giving include texts worth reading and tasks worth doing. Ideally, time spent on such formative assessments shouldn't be time lost to instruction but rather an opportunity both for students to demonstrate what they have learned as well as a chance for additional practice.

Malcolm Gladwell estimates in his book *Outliers* that mastering a skill requires about 10,000 hours of dedicated practice. He argues that individuals who are outstanding in their field have one thing in common—many, many hours of working at it. Gladwell claims that success is less dependent on innate talent than it is on practice. Now I'm pretty sure that I could put in 10,000 hours at a ballet studio and still be a terrible dancer, but I agree with Gladwell that, "Practice isn't the thing you do once you're good. It's the thing you do that makes you good."

Not just any kind of practice will help students meet English Language Arts Standards, though. Effective practice needs to focus on improvement. That is why this series of reading and writing tasks begins with a model of the kind of reading and writing students are working towards, then takes them through practice exercises, and finally invites them to perform the skills they have practiced.

Once through the cycle is only the beginning. You will want your students to repeat the process several times over until close reading, supporting claims with evidence, and crafting a compelling essay is something they approach with confidence. Notice that I didn't say "with ease." I wish it were otherwise, but in my experience as a teacher and as an author, writing well is never easy.

I hope you find these assessment tools a valuable, seamless addition to a standards-aligned curriculum.

Unit 1 Argumentative Essay
Animal and Human Interactions

Unit 2 Informative Essay
Disaster!

Unit 3 Literary Analysis
Making Choices

Unit 4 Mixed Practice
On Your Own

Animal and Human Interactions

STEP 1 ANALYZE THE MODEL

Should animals be kept in zoos?

Page 5
Discuss and Decide

As students discuss whether or not animals should be kept in zoos, remind them to cite textual evidence.

Page 7
Discuss and Decide

As students discuss whether the student model convinced them that zoos are worthwhile, remind them to cite textual evidence.

Page 8
Terminology of Argumentative Texts

Accept reasonable responses that demonstrate comprehension of the terms and their application to the texts.

STEP 2 PRACTICE THE TASK

Should people be allowed to keep pit bulls as pets?

Page 10
Close Read

Student answers should demonstrate comprehension and draw evidence from the text. They may cite that Goodman states that when pit bulls grab on they don't let go, and that they are the breed of choice for drug dealers and "other bad folks."

Page 11
Discuss and Decide

As students discuss what the article suggests some pit bull owners will need to do, such as moving to another county if they want to own pit bulls, remind them to cite textual evidence.

Page 12
Discuss and Decide

As students discuss the reasons the blog gives for the enduring popularity of pit bulls and why a pit bull might make a good pet, remind them to cite textual evidence.

Page 13
Close Read

1. Student answers should demonstrate comprehension and draw evidence from the text. They may include the author's claim that the media only cover dog attacks that include pit bulls and the fact that he cites the ASPCA as an expert source.

2. Student answers should demonstrate comprehension and draw evidence from the text. They may state that *over-report* means that pit bulls get more coverage by the media than other dogs. They may include that attacks by dogs of unknown breeds are attributed to pit bulls.

Page 14
Respond to Questions on Step 2 Sources

1. Accept responses that demonstrate comprehension and draw evidence from the source. Reputable newspapers check their sources, so it is likely that the information is accurate. Blogs and editorials represent personal opinions and may or may not be accurate.

2. Prose Constructed-Response

   Scoring Notes: Use the rubric to evaluate student responses. Responses may include but are not limited to:

   - The newspaper article on Dade County keeping the ban on pit bulls provides the most credible evidence in support of banning pit bull ownership.

   - Dade County continues to recognize that a pit bull attack of a child can cause long-term injuries.

2	The response gives sufficient evidence of the ability to evaluate the credibility, completeness, relevancy, and/or accuracy of the information and sources.
1	The response gives limited evidence of the ability to evaluate the credibility, completeness, relevancy, and/or accuracy of the information and sources.
0	A response gets no credit if it provides no evidence of the ability to evaluate the credibility, completeness, relevancy, and/or accuracy of the information and sources.

3. Prose Constructed-Response

   Scoring Notes: Use the rubric to evaluate student responses. Responses may include but are not limited to:

   - Some breeds have more reported incidences of attacks, but not all attacks are reported.

   - Ohio's laws make the label of *dangerous* or *vicious* dog-specific, not breed-specific.

2	The response gives sufficient evidence of the ability to evaluate the credibility, completeness, relevancy, and/or accuracy of the information and sources.
1	The response gives limited evidence of the ability to evaluate the credibility, completeness, relevancy, and/or accuracy of the information and sources.
0	A response gets no credit if it provides no evidence of the ability to evaluate the credibility, completeness, relevancy, and/or accuracy of the information and sources.

Pages 16–18
Planning and Prewriting

Review and critique students' planning documents; offer feedback as needed.

Pages 19–20
Argumentative Essay

Scoring Notes: Use the rubric to evaluate student responses.

	Development of Ideas	Organization	Clarity of Language	Language and Conventions
4	The response addresses the prompt and shows effective and comprehensive development of the claimusing text-based evidence, clear and convincing reasoning, and/or description.	The response demonstrates coherence and clarity and a logical organization that includes an introduction and conclusion and a logical progression of ideas.	The response establishes and maintains an effective style, including precise language, descriptive words and phrases, transitional words and phrases, and domain-specific vocabulary.	The response demonstrates a command of standard English conventions consistent with effectively edited writing.
3	The response addresses the prompt and shows effective development of the topic using text-based evidence, reasoning, and/or description.	The response demonstrates some logical organization and includes an introduction and conclusion.	Some descriptive words, as well as some linking words and phrases, are used to express ideas with clarity.	The response demonstrates a command of standard English conventions, although there may be some minor errors in grammar and usage.

	Development of Ideas	Organization	Clarity of Language	Language and Conventions
2	The response addresses the prompt and shows some development of the topic but fails to use text-based evidence, reasoning, and/or description.	The response demonstrates little logical organization and includes either an introduction or a conclusion.	Few descriptive words, as well as a few linking words and phrases, are used and ideas are not expressed as clearly as possible.	The response demonstrates a command of standard English conventions, although there are major errors in grammar and usage.
1	The response does not directly address the prompt, shows no development of the topic, and fails to use text-based evidence, reasoning, and/or description.	The response demonstrates little logical organization and fails to includes either an introduction or a conclusion.	No descriptive words or linking words and phrases are used and ideas are not expressed with clarity.	Errors in grammar and usage create confusion of meaning.
0	No evidence of the ability to write an argumentative essay.			

STEP 3 PERFORM THE TASK

Can animals learn or use language?

Page 23
Close Read

Student answers should demonstrate comprehension and draw evidence from the text. They may include that Kanzi points to appropriate symbols on his keyboard in response to a spoken word and responds appropriately to commands.

Page 25
Discuss and Decide

As students discuss Kanzi's communication abilities, remind them to cite textual evidence.

Page 27
Close Read

Student answers should demonstrate comprehension and draw evidence from the text. They may include that natural animal communications lack displacement, discreteness, and or productivity.

Page 28
Discuss and Decide

As students discuss the difference between language and communication and the part communication plays in the broader understanding of language, remind them to cite textual evidence.

Page 29
Respond to Questions on Step 3 Sources

1. c.

2. c.

3. c.

4. b.

Page 30

5. Accept responses that demonstrate comprehension and draw evidence from the source. Reputable magazines check their sources, so it is likely that the information is accurate. The graphic feature may or may not be credible—no source is given.

6. Prose Constructed-Response

Scoring Notes: Use the rubric to evaluate student responses. Responses may include but are not include but are not limited to:

- Some animals learn to understand and respond to human language.
- Understanding and responding to human language is not the same as communicating.

2	The response gives sufficient evidence of the ability to evaluate the credibility, completeness, relevancy, and/or accuracy of the information and sources.
1	The response gives limited evidence of the ability to evaluate the credibility, completeness, relevancy, and/or accuracy of the information and sources.
0	A response gets no credit if it provides no evidence of the ability to evaluate the credibility, completeness, relevancy, and/or accuracy of the information and sources.

Pages 31–32
Argumentative Essay

Scoring Notes: Use the rubric to evaluate student responses.

	Development of Ideas	Organization	Clarity of Language	Language and Conventions
4	The response addresses the prompt and shows effective and comprehensive development of the claimusing text-based evidence, clear and convincing reasoning, and/or description.	The response demonstrates coherence and clarity, a logical organization that includes an introduction and conclusion, and a logical progression of ideas.	The response establishes and maintains an effective style, including precise language, descriptive words and phrases, transitional words and phrases, and domain-specific vocabulary.	The response demonstrates a command of standard English conventions consistent with effectively edited writing.
3	The response addresses the prompt and shows effective development of the topic using text-based evidence, reasoning, and/or description.	The response demonstrates some logical organization and includes an introduction and conclusion.	Some descriptive words, as well as some linking words and phrases, are used to express ideas with clarity.	The response demonstrates a command of standard English conventions, although there may be some minor errors in grammar and usage.
2	The response addresses the prompt and shows some development of the topic but fails to use text-based evidence, reasoning, and/or description.	The response demonstrates little logical organization and includes either an introduction or a conclusion.	Few descriptive words, as well as a few linking words and phrases, are used and ideas are not expressed as clearly as possible.	The response demonstrates a command of standard English conventions, although there are major errors in grammar and usage.

	Development of Ideas	Organization	Clarity of Language	Language and Conventions
1	The response does not directly address the prompt and shows no development of the topic and fails to use text-based evidence, reasoning, and/or description.	The response demonstrates little logical organization and fails to includes either an introduction or a conclusion.	No descriptive words or linking words and phrases are used and ideas are not expressed with clarity.	Errors in grammar and usage create confusion of meaning.
0	No evidence of the ability to write an argumentative essay.			

Disaster!

STEP 1 ANALYZE THE MODEL

What causes home fires and how can we prevent them?

Page 37
Discuss and Decide

As students discuss which pattern of organization seems most appropriate for the topic, remind them to cite textual evidence.

Page 39
Discuss and Decide

As students discuss how the information about clothes dryers relates to Robert's main idea, remind them to cite textual evidence.

Page 41
Discuss and Decide

As students discuss whether the descriptive language added or took away from their understanding of the fires' causes and effects, remind them to cite textual evidence.

Page 42
Terminology of Informative Essays

Accept reasonable responses that demonstrate comprehension of the terms and their application to the texts.

STEP 2 PRACTICE THE TASK

How are hurricanes and tornadoes alike and different?

Page 47
Discuss and Decide

As students discuss whether the essay or the map gives them a better understanding of what parts of the United States face tornadoes, remind them to cite textual evidence.

Page 49
Discuss and Decide

As students discuss whether they have gathered more information about tornadoes or hurricanes from the sources, remind them to cite textual evidence.

Page 50
Respond to Questions on Step 2 Sources

1. c.

2. b.

3. c.

Page 51
4. a.

5. d.

6. Prose Constructed-Response

Scoring Notes: Use the rubric to evaluate student responses. Responses may include but are not limited to:

• The main idea and supporting details of the section "Size Versus Impact" in "What You Should Know about Tornadoes."

2	The response gives sufficient evidence of the ability to cite evidence to support arguments and/or ideas.
1	The response gives limited evidence of the ability to cite evidence to support arguments and/or ideas.
0	A response gets no credit if it provides no evidence of the ability to cite evidence to support arguments and/or ideas.

7. Prose Constructed-Response

Scoring Notes: Use the rubric to evaluate student responses. Responses may include but are not limited to:

• Information from the map about how hurricanes form.

• Information from the text in "Basic Facts About Hurricanes" about how hurricanes form.

2	The response gives sufficient evidence of the ability to evaluate the credibility, completeness, relevancy, and/or accuracy of the information and sources.
1	The response gives limited evidence of the ability to evaluate the credibility, completeness, relevancy, and/or accuracy of the information and sources.
0	A response gets no credit if it provides no evidence of the ability to evaluate the credibility, completeness, relevancy, and/or accuracy of the information and sources.

Pages 52–54
Planning and Prewriting

Review and critique students' planning documents; offer feedback as needed.

Pages 55–56
Informative Essay

Scoring Notes: Use the rubric to evaluate student responses.

	Development of Ideas	Organization	Clarity of Language	Language and Conventions
4	The response addresses the prompt and shows effective and comprehensive development of the controlling idea using text-based evidence, clear and convincing reasoning, and/or description.	The response demonstrates coherence and clarity, a logical organization that includes an introduction and conclusion, and a logical progression of ideas.	The response establishes and maintains an effective style, including precise language, descriptive words and phrases, transitional words and phrases, and domain-specific vocabulary.	The response demonstrates a command of standard English conventions consistent with effectively edited writing.
3	The response addresses the prompt and shows effective development of the topic using text-based evidence, reasoning, and/or description.	The response demonstrates some logical organization and includes an introduction and conclusion.	Some descriptive words, as well as some linking words and phrases, are used to express ideas with clarity.	The response demonstrates a command of standard English conventions, although there may be some minor errors in grammar and usage.
2	The response addresses the prompt and shows some development of the topic but fails to use text-based evidence, reasoning, and/or description.	The response demonstrates little logical organization and includes either an introduction or a conclusion.	Few descriptive words, as well as a few linking words and phrases, are used and ideas are not expressed as clearly as possible.	The response demonstrates a command of standard English conventions, although there are major errors in grammar and usage.

	Development of Ideas	Organization	Clarity of Language	Language and Conventions
1	The response does not directly address the prompt, shows no development of the topic, and fails to use text-based evidence, reasoning, and/or description.	The response demonstrates little logical organization and fails to include either an introduction or a conclusion.	No descriptive words or linking words and phrases are used and ideas are not expressed with clarity.	Errors in grammar and usage create confusion of meaning.
0	No evidence of the ability to write an informative essay.			

STEP 3 PERFORM THE TASK

How are rogue waves and tsunamis alike and different?

Page 59
Discuss and Decide

As students discuss what information about the Bermuda Triangle hints at an explanation of the origin of rogue waves, remind them to cite textual evidence.

Page 60
Close Read

Student answers should demonstrate comprehension and draw evidence from the text. They may cite how a storm surge is different from a rogue wave, including how a rogue wave only occurs far out at sea.

Page 62
Discuss and Decide

As students discuss whether a rogue wave can be considered a tsunami and why or why not, remind them to cite textual evidence.

Page 63
Respond to Questions on Step 3 Sources

1. a.

2. d.

3. c.

4. d.

Page 64

5. Prose Constructed-Response

Scoring Notes: Use the rubric to evaluate student responses. Responses may include but are not limited to:

- Information about how earthquakes trigger tsunamis, using details from "What Causes Tsunamis?"

- Information about how landslides trigger tsunamis, using details from "What Causes Tsunamis?"

2	The response gives sufficient evidence of the ability to cite evidence to support arguments and/or ideas.
1	The response gives limited evidence of the ability to cite evidence to support arguments and/or ideas.
0	A response gets no credit if it provides no evidence of the ability to cite evidence to support arguments and/or ideas.

6. Prose Constructed-Response

Scoring Notes: Use the rubric to evaluate student responses. Responses may include but are not limited to:

- The main idea and supporting details of the section "Why So High?" in "What Are Rogue Waves?"

2	The response gives sufficient evidence of the ability to evaluate the credibility, completeness, relevancy, and/or accuracy of the information and sources.
1	The response gives limited evidence of the ability to evaluate the credibility, completeness, relevancy, and/or accuracy of the information and sources.
0	A response gets no credit if it provides no evidence of the ability to evaluate the credibility, completeness, relevancy, and/or accuracy of the information and sources.

7. Prose Constructed-Response

Scoring Notes: Use the rubric to evaluate student responses. Responses may include but are not limited to:

- Information from "What Are Rogue Waves?" about the importance of the Bermuda Triangle to rogue waves.

2	The response gives sufficient evidence of the ability to evaluate the credibility, completeness, relevancy, and/or accuracy of the information and sources.
1	The response gives limited evidence of the ability to evaluate the credibility, completeness, relevancy, and/or accuracy of the information and sources.
0	A response gets no credit if it provides no evidence of the ability to evaluate the credibility, completeness, relevancy, and/or accuracy of the information and sources.

Pages 65–66
Informative Essay
Scoring Notes: Use the rubric to evaluate student responses.

	Development of Ideas	**Organization**	**Clarity of Language**	**Language and Conventions**
4	The response addresses the prompt and shows effective and comprehensive development of the controlling idea using text-based evidence, clear and convincing reasoning, and/or description.	The response demonstrates coherence and clarity, a logical organization that includes an introduction and conclusion, and a logical progression of ideas.	The response establishes and maintains an effective style, including precise language, descriptive words and phrases, transitional words and phrases, and domain-specific vocabulary.	The response demonstrates a command of standard English conventions consistent with effectively edited writing.
3	The response addresses the prompt and shows effective development of the topic using text-based evidence, reasoning, and/or description.	The response demonstrates some logical organization and includes an introduction and conclusion.	Some descriptive words, as well as some linking words and phrases, are used to express ideas with clarity.	The response demonstrates a command of standard English conventions, although there may be some minor errors in grammar and usage.

	Development of Ideas	Organization	Clarity of Language	Language and Conventions
2	The response addresses the prompt and shows some development of the topic but fails to use text-based evidence, reasoning, and/or description.	The response demonstrates little logical organization and includes either an introduction or a conclusion.	Few descriptive words, as well as a few linking words and phrases, are used and ideas are not expressed as clearly as possible.	The response demonstrates a command of standard English conventions, although there are major errors in grammar and usage.
1	The response does not directly address the prompt, shows no development of the topic, and fails to use text-based evidence, reasoning, and/or description.	The response demonstrates little logical organization and fails to include either an introduction or a conclusion.	No descriptive words or linking words and phrases are used and ideas are not expressed with clarity.	Errors in grammar and usage create confusion of meaning.
0	No evidence of the ability to write an informative essay.			

Viewpoints

STEP 1 ANALYZE THE MODEL

How do others view us?

Page 71
Discuss and Decide

As students review David's notes and discuss why the ending of each poem is ironic, remind them to cite textual evidence.

Page 73
Discuss and Decide

As students discuss how the view of the Earth's destruction in the poems is different from what they might expect, remind them to cite textual evidence.

Page 74
Terminology of Literary Analysis

Accept reasonable responses that demonstrate comprehension of the terms and their application to the texts.

STEP 2 PRACTICE THE TASK

How does the information we have affect our viewpoint?

Page 77
Discuss and Decide

As students discuss which actions in the folk tale about the mysterious visitor convey the lesson that it is important to be kind to people, remind them to cite textual evidence.

Page 79
Discuss and Decide

As students discuss in a small group why all of the men are "in the wrong," remind them to cite textual evidence.

Page 81
Discuss and Decide

As students discuss in a small group why each of the friends has a different view of the coat, remind them to cite textual evidence.

Page 82
Respond to Questions on Step 2 Sources

1. c.

2. c.

3. a.

Page 83
4. Prose Constructed-Response

Scoring Notes: Use the rubric to evaluate student responses. Responses may include but are not limited to:

• Information about what the first blind man thinks about the elephant.

• Information about what the second blind man thinks about the elephant.

• Information about what the third man thinks about the elephant.

2	The response gives sufficient evidence of the ability to cite evidence to support arguments and/or ideas.
1	The response gives limited evidence of the ability to cite evidence to support arguments and/or ideas.
0	A response gets no credit if it provides no evidence of the ability to cite evidence to support arguments and/or ideas.

5. Prose Constructed-Response

Scoring Notes: Use the rubric to evaluate student responses. Responses may include but are not limited to:

• Information about the reactions of the blind men in "Six Men and an Elephant."

• Information about the reactions of the boys in "The Red and Blue Coat."

2	The response gives sufficient evidence of the ability to gather, analyze, and integrate information within and among multiple sources of information.
1	The response gives limited evidence of the ability to gather, analyze, and integrate information within and among multiple sources of information.
0	A response gets no credit if it provides no evidence of the ability to gather, analyze, and integrate information within and among multiple sources of information.

6. Prose Constructed-Response

Scoring Notes: Use the rubric to evaluate student responses. Responses may include but are not limited to:

- Information about the way the blind men perceive events in "Six Men and an Elephant."
- Information about the way the boys perceive events in "The Red and Blue Coat."

2	The response gives sufficient evidence of the ability to gather, analyze, and integrate information within and among multiple sources of information.
1	The response gives limited evidence of the ability to gather, analyze, and integrate information within and among multiple sources of information.
0	A response gets no credit if it provides no evidence of the ability to gather, analyze, and integrate information within and among multiple sources of information.

Pages 84–86
Planning and Prewriting

Review and critique students' planning documents; offer feedback as needed.

Pages 87–88
Literary Analysis

Scoring Notes: Use the rubric to evaluate student responses.

	Development of Ideas	Organization	Clarity of Language	Language and Conventions
4	The response addresses the prompt and shows effective and comprehensive development of the controlling idea using text-based evidence, clear and convincing reasoning, and/or description.	The response demonstrates coherence and clarity, a logical organization that includes an introduction and conclusion, and a logical progression of ideas.	The response establishes and maintains an effective style, including precise language, descriptive words and phrases, transitional words and phrases, and domain-specific vocabulary.	The response demonstrates a command of standard English conventions consistent with effectively edited writing.

	Development of Ideas	Organization	Clarity of Language	Language and Conventions
3	The response addresses the prompt and shows effective development of the topic using text-based evidence, reasoning, and/or description.	The response demonstrates some logical organization and includes an introduction and conclusion.	Some descriptive words, as well as some linking words and phrases, are used to express ideas with clarity.	The response demonstrates a command of standard English conventions, although there may be some minor errors in grammar and usage.
2	The response addresses the prompt and shows some development of the topic but fails to use text-based evidence, reasoning, and/or description.	The response demonstrates little logical organization and includes either an introduction or a conclusion.	Few descriptive words, as well as a few linking words and phrases, are used and ideas are not expressed as clearly as possible.	The response demonstrates a command of standard English conventions, although there are major errors in grammar and usage.
1	The response does not directly address the prompt, shows no development of the topic, and fails to use text-based evidence, reasoning, and/or description.	The response demonstrates little logical organization and fails to include either an introduction or a conclusion.	No descriptive words or linking words and phrases are used and ideas are not expressed with clarity.	Errors in grammar and usage create confusion of meaning.
0	No evidence of the ability to write a literary analysis.			

STEP 3 PERFORM THE TASK

How can the theme of a story convey a viewpoint about life?

Page 91
Discuss and Decide

As students discuss with a partner ways in which authors develop theme and how title, plot, characters, and other literary elements convey the theme, remind them to cite textual evidence.

Page 93

Discuss and Decide

As students discuss in a small group why the narrator lies to Miss Crosman, remind them to cite textual evidence.

Page 95

Discuss and Decide

As students discuss with a partner their impressions of Miss Crosman, remind them to cite textual evidence.

Page 96

Discuss and Decide

As students discuss with a partner why the narrator learned to play a second, more difficult piece, remind them to cite textual evidence.

Page 98

Discuss and Decide

As students compare and contrast in a small group the sisters' words and actions and how they feel about their mother's having to be at work, remind them to cite textual evidence.

Page 100

Discuss and Decide

As students discuss with a small group what the umbrella really means to the narrator and whether owning it will change anything for her, remind them to cite textual evidence.

Page 102

Close Read

Student answers should demonstrate comprehension and draw evidence from the text. They may cite what larger lesson about life or human nature the narrator might have learned and what this action suggests about the theme of the story, such as the theme that possessions are not important.

Page 103

Respond to Questions on Step 3 Sources

1. b.

2. c.

3. a.

4. d.

Respond to Questions on Step 3 Sources

Page 104

5. Prose Constructed-Response

Scoring Notes: Use the rubric to evaluate student responses. Responses
may include but are not limited to:

- Analysis of why the narrator lies about her mother's job.

- Analysis of what the narrator's lies reveal about her feelings.

2	The response gives sufficient evidence of the ability to cite evidence to support arguments and/or ideas.
1	The response gives limited evidence of the ability to cite evidence to support arguments and/or ideas.
0	A response gets no credit if it provides no evidence of the ability to cite evidence to support arguments and/or ideas.

6. Prose Constructed-Response

Scoring Notes: Use the rubric to evaluate student responses. Responses
may include but are not limited to:

- Analysis of what the white umbrella represents.

- Analysis of what the white umbrella suggests about the theme.

2	The response gives sufficient evidence of the ability to cite evidence to support arguments and/or ideas.
1	The response gives limited evidence of the ability to cite evidence to support arguments and/or ideas.
0	A response gets no credit if it provides no evidence of the ability to cite evidence to support arguments and/or ideas.

7. Prose Constructed-Response

Scoring Notes: Use the rubric to evaluate student responses. Responses
may include but are not limited to:

- Analysis of how the accident relates to the narrator's feelings about her
  mother.

- Analysis of how the accident relates to the theme.

2	The response gives sufficient evidence of the ability to cite evidence to support arguments and/or ideas.
1	The response gives limited evidence of the ability to cite evidence to support arguments and/or ideas.
0	A response gets no credit if it provides no evidence of the ability to cite evidence to support arguments and/or ideas.

Pages 105–106
Literary Analysis

Scoring Notes: Use the rubric to evaluate student responses.

	Development of Ideas	Organization	Clarity of Language	Language and Conventions
4	The response addresses the prompt and shows effective and comprehensive development of the controlling idea using text-based evidence, clear and convincing reasoning, and/or description.	The response demonstrates coherence and clarity, a logical organization that includes an introduction and conclusion, and a logical progression of ideas.	The response establishes and maintains an effective style, including precise language, descriptive words and phrases, transitional words and phrases, and domain-specific vocabulary.	The response demonstrates a command of standard English conventions consistent with effectively edited writing.
3	The response addresses the prompt and shows effective development of the topic using text-based evidence, reasoning, and/or description.	The response demonstrates some logical organization and includes an introduction and conclusion.	Some descriptive words, as well as some linking words and phrases, are used to express ideas with clarity.	The response demonstrates a command of standard English conventions, although there may be some minor errors in grammar and usage.

© Houghton Mifflin Harcourt Publishing Company

	Development of Ideas	Organization	Clarity of Language	Language and Conventions
2	The response addresses the prompt and shows some development of the topic but fails to use text-based evidence, reasoning, and/or description.	The response demonstrates little logical organization and includes either an introduction or a conclusion.	Few descriptive words, as well as a few linking words and phrases, are used and ideas are not expressed as clearly as possible.	The response demonstrates a command of standard English conventions, although there are major errors in grammar and usage.
1	The response does not directly address the prompt, shows no development of the topic, and fails to use text-based evidence, reasoning, and/or description.	The response demonstrates little logical organization and fails to include either an introduction or a conclusion.	No descriptive words or linking words and phrases are used and ideas are not expressed with clarity.	Errors in grammar and usage create confusion of meaning.
0	No evidence of the ability to write a literary analysis.			

On Your Own

TASK 1 ARGUMENTATIVE ESSAY

Page 118

1. c.

2. Prose Constructed-Response

Scoring Notes: Use the rubric to evaluate student responses. Responses may include but are not limited to:

- The Obama administration believed that a day-long conference on bullying was needed because bullying is "a school safety issue." Education Secretary Arne Duncan said that bullying "is doubly dangerous because if left unattended, it can rapidly escalate into even more serious violence and abuse."

- The primary goal of the conference was to refute "the belief that bullying is a normal rite of passage" and also to "share ideas about how the federal government and communities can help prevent bullying."

2	The response gives sufficient evidence of the ability to cite evidence to support arguments and/or ideas.
1	The response gives limited evidence of the ability to cite evidence to support arguments and/or ideas.
0	A response gets no credit if it provides no evidence of the ability to cite evidence to support arguments and/or ideas.

3. Prose Constructed-Response

Scoring Notes: Use the rubric to evaluate student responses. Responses may include but are not limited to:

- Advice given to parents of a bully includes accepting that there is a problem, getting advice from school counselors or other professionals, having an open dialogue with the child, monitoring the child, withdrawing privileges from the child and replacing the privileges with positive activities, developing strategies to deal with anger, having the child apologize to victims, and modeling proper behavior.

2	The response gives sufficient evidence of the ability to cite evidence to support arguments and/or ideas.
1	The response gives limited evidence of the ability to cite evidence to support arguments and/or ideas.
0	A response gets no credit if it provides no evidence of the ability to cite evidence to support arguments and/or ideas.

10-Point Argumentative Performance Task Writing Rubric (Grades 6–11)

Scoring Notes: This ten-point rubric is composed of three traits: Organization/Purpose, Evidence/Elaboration, and Conventions. Evaluate student responses using the criteria from each of the three traits and add the individual scores together to arrive at an overall score point value.

4-Point Argumentative Performance Task Writing Rubric (Grades 6–11)				
Score	**Organization/Purpose**			
4	The response has a clear and effective organizational structure, creating a sense of unity and completeness. The organization is fully sustained between and within paragraphs. The response is consistently and purposefully focused:			
	• claim is introduced, clearly communicated, and the focus is strongly maintained for the purpose and audience	• consistent use of a variety of transitional strategies to clarify the relationships between and among ideas	• effective introduction and conclusion	• logical progression of ideas from beginning to end; strong connections between and among ideas with some syntactic variety	• alternate and opposing argument(s) are clearly acknowledged or addressed*
3	The response has an evident organizational structure and a sense of completeness. Though there may be minor flaws, they do not interfere with the overall coherence. The organization is adequately sustained between and within paragraphs. The response is generally focused:			
	• claim is clear, and the focus is mostly maintained for the purpose and audience	• adequate use of transitional strategies with some variety to clarify relationships between and among ideas	• adequate introduction and conclusion	• adequate progression of ideas from beginning to end; adequate connections between and among ideas	• alternate and opposing argument(s) are adequately acknowledged or addressed*

* Acknowledging and/or addressing the opposing point of view begins at grade 7.

2	The response has an inconsistent organizational structure. Some flaws are evident, and some ideas may be loosely connected. The organization is somewhat sustained between and within paragraphs. The response may have a minor drift in focus:				
	• claim may be somewhat unclear, or the focus may be insufficiently sustained for the purpose and/or audience	• inconsistent use of transitional strategies and/or little variety	• introduction or conclusion, if present, may be weak	• uneven progression of ideas from beginning to end; and/or formulaic; inconsistent or unclear connections among ideas	• alternate and opposing argument(s) may be confusing or not acknowledged*
1	The response has little or no discernible organizational structure. The response may be related to the claim but may provide little or no focus:				
	• claim may be confusing or ambiguous; response may be too brief or the focus may drift from the purpose and/or audience	• few or no transitional strategies are evident	• introduction and/or conclusion may be missing	• frequent extraneous ideas may be evident; ideas may be randomly ordered or have unclear progression	• alternate and opposing argument(s) may not be acknowledged*
NS	• Insufficient (includes copied text)	• In a language other than English	• Off-topic	• Off-purpose	

* Acknowledging and/or addressing the opposing point of view begins at grade 7.

4-Point Argumentative Performance Task Writing Rubric (Grades 6–11)				
Score	**Evidence/Elaboration**			
4	The response provides thorough and convincing elaboration of the support/evidence for the claim and argument(s) including reasoned, in-depth analysis and the effective use of source material. The response clearly and effectively develops ideas, using precise language:			
	• comprehensive evidence (facts and details) from the source material is integrated, relevant, and specific	• clear citations or attribution to source material	• effective use of a variety of elaborative techniques*	• vocabulary is clearly appropriate for the audience and purpose	• effective, appropriate style enhances content
3	The response provides adequate elaboration of the support/evidence for the claim and argument(s) that includes reasoned analysis and the use of source material. The response adequately develops ideas, employing a mix of precise with more general language:			
	• adequate evidence (facts and details) from the source material is integrated and relevant, yet may be general	• adequate use of citations or attribution to source material	• adequate use of some elaborative techniques*	• vocabulary is generally appropriate for the audience and purpose	• generally appropriate style is evident

* Elaborative techniques may include the use of personal experiences that support the argument(s).

2	The response provides uneven, cursory elaboration of the support/evidence for the claim and argument(s) that includes some reasoned analysis and partial or uneven use of source material. The response develops ideas unevenly, using simplistic language:				
	• some evidence (facts and details) from the source material may be weakly integrated, imprecise, repetitive, vague, and/or copied	• weak use of citations or attribution to source material	• weak or uneven use of elaborative techniques*; development may consist primarily of source summary or may rely on emotional appeal	• vocabulary use is uneven or somewhat ineffective for the audience and purpose	• inconsistent or weak attempt to create appropriate style
1	The response provides minimal elaboration of the support/evidence for the claim and argument(s) that includes little or no use of source material. The response is vague, lacks clarity, or is confusing:				
	• evidence (facts and details) from the source material is minimal, irrelevant, absent, incorrectly used, or predominantly copied	• insufficient use of citations or attribution to source material	• minimal, if any, use of elaborative techniques*; emotional appeal may dominate	• vocabulary is limited or ineffective for the audience and purpose	• little or no evidence of appropriate style
NS	• Insufficient (includes copied text)	• In a language other than English	• Off-topic	• Off-purpose	

* Elaborative techniques may include the use of personal experiences that support the argument(s).

	2-Point Argumentative Performance Task Writing Rubric (Grades 6–11)			
Score	**Conventions**			
2	**The response demonstrates an adequate command of conventions:**			
	• adequate use of correct sentence formation, punctuation, capitalization, grammar usage, and spelling			
1	**The response demonstrates a partial command of conventions:**			
	• limited use of correct sentence formation, punctuation, capitalization, grammar usage, and spelling			
0	**The response demonstrates little or no command of conventions:**			
	• infrequent use of correct sentence formation, punctuation, capitalization, grammar usage, and spelling			
NS	• Insufficient (includes copied text)	• In a language other than English	• Off-topic	• Off-purpose

Holistic Scoring:

- **Variety:** A range of errors includes sentence formation, punctuation, capitalization, grammar usage, and spelling.

- **Severity:** Basic errors are more heavily weighted than higher-level errors.

- **Density:** The proportion of errors to the amount of writing done well. This includes the ratio of errors to the length of the piece.

TASK 2 INFORMATIVE ESSAY

Page 133

1. Prose Constructed-Response

Scoring Notes: Use the rubric to evaluate student responses. Responses may include but are not limited to:

- The surface of the bike trail should be safe for riding.
- The trail should have pleasing scenery.
- The terrain should not be too difficult.
- The trail should be easy to get to.
- Text evidence must be provided for all of the above points.

2	The response gives sufficient evidence of the ability to cite evidence to support arguments and/or ideas.
1	The response gives limited evidence of the ability to cite evidence to support arguments and/or ideas.
0	A response gets no credit if it provides no evidence of the ability to cite evidence to support arguments and/or ideas.

2. d.

Page 134

3. a.

10-Point Explanatory Performance Task Writing Rubric (Grades 6–11)

Scoring Notes: This ten-point rubric is composed of three traits: Organization/Purpose, Evidence/Elaboration, and Conventions. Evaluate student responses using the criteria from each of the three traits and add the individual scores together to arrive at an overall score point value.

4-Point Explanatory Performance Task Writing Rubric (Grades 6–11)				
Score	**Organization/Purpose**			
4	The response has a clear and effective organizational structure, creating a sense of unity and completeness. The organization is fully sustained between and within paragraphs. The response is consistently and purposefully focused:			
	• thesis/controlling idea of a topic is clearly communicated, and the focus is strongly maintained for the purpose and audience	• consistent use of a variety of transitional strategies to clarify the relationships between and among ideas	• effective introduction and conclusion	• logical progression of ideas from beginning to end; strong connections between and among ideas with some syntactic variety
3	The response has an evident organizational structure and a sense of completeness. Though there may be minor flaws, they do not interfere with the overall coherence. The organization is adequately sustained between and within paragraphs. The response is generally focused:			
	• thesis/controlling idea of a topic is clear, and the focus is mostly maintained for the purpose and audience	• adequate use of transitional strategies with some variety to clarify the relationships between and among ideas	• adequate introduction and conclusion	• adequate progression of ideas from beginning to end; adequate connections between and among ideas

2	The response has an inconsistent organizational structure. Some flaws are evident, and some ideas may be loosely connected. The organization is somewhat sustained between and within paragraphs. The response may have a minor drift in focus:			
	• thesis/controlling idea of a topic may be somewhat unclear, or the focus may be insufficiently sustained for the purpose and/or audience	• inconsistent use of transitional strategies and/or little variety	• introduction or conclusion, if present, may be weak	• uneven progression of ideas from beginning to end; and/or formulaic; inconsistent or unclear connections between and among ideas
1	The response has little or no discernible organizational structure. The response may be related to the claim but may provide little or no focus:			
	• thesis/controlling idea may be confusing or ambiguous; response may be too brief or the focus may drift from the purpose and/or audience	• few or no transitional strategies are evident	• introduction and/or conclusion may be missing	• frequent extraneous ideas may be evident; ideas may be randomly ordered or have an unclear progression
NS	• Insufficient (includes copied text)	• In a language other than English	• Off-topic	• Off-purpose

Score	Evidence/Elaboration				
	4-Point Explanatory Performance Task Writing Rubric (Grades 6–11)				
4	The response provides thorough elaboration of the support/evidence for the thesis/controlling idea that includes the effective use of source material. The response clearly and effectively develops ideas, using precise language:				
	• comprehensive evidence (facts and details) from the source material is integrated, relevant, and specific	• clear citations or attribution to source material	• effective use of a variety of elaborative techniques*	• vocabulary is clearly appropriate for the audience and purpose	• effective, appropriate style enhances content
3	The response provides adequate elaboration of the support/evidence for the thesis/controlling idea that includes the use of source material. The response adequately develops ideas, employing a mix of precise and more general language:				
	• adequate evidence (facts and details) from the source material is integrated and relevant, yet may be general	• adequate use of citations or attribution to source material	• adequate use of some elaborative techniques*	• vocabulary is generally appropriate for the audience and purpose	• generally appropriate style is evident

* Elaborative techniques may include the use of personal experiences that support the thesis/controlling idea.

2	The response provides uneven, cursory elaboration of the support/evidence for the thesis/controlling idea that includes uneven or limited use of source material. The response develops ideas unevenly, using simplistic language:				
	• some evidence (facts and details) from the source material may be weakly integrated, imprecise, repetitive, vague, and/or copied	• weak use of citations or attribution to source material	• weak or uneven use of elaborative techniques*; development may consist primarily of source summary	• vocabulary use is uneven or somewhat ineffective for the audience and purpose	• inconsistent or weak attempt to create appropriate style
1	The response provides minimal elaboration of the support/evidence for the thesis/controlling idea that includes little or no use of source material. The response is vague, lacks clarity, or is confusing:				
	• evidence (facts and details) from the source material is minimal, irrelevant, absent, incorrectly used, or predominantly copied	• insufficient use of citations or attribution to source material	• minimal, if any, use of elaborative techniques*	• vocabulary is limited or ineffective for the audience and purpose	• little or no evidence of appropriate style
NS	• Insufficient (includes copied text)	• In a language other than English	• Off-topic	• Off-purpose	

* Elaborative techniques may include the use of personal experiences that support the thesis/controlling idea.

	2-Point Explanatory Performance Task Writing Rubric (Grades 6–11)			
Score	**Conventions**			
2	**The response demonstrates an adequate command of conventions:**			
	• adequate use of correct sentence formation, punctuation, capitalization, grammar usage, and spelling			
1	**The response demonstrates a partial command of conventions:**			
	• limited use of correct sentence formation, punctuation, capitalization, grammar usage, and spelling			
0	**The response demonstrates little or no command of conventions:**			
	• infrequent use of correct sentence formation, punctuation, capitalization, grammar usage, and spelling			
NS	• Insufficient (includes copied text)	• In a language other than English	• Off-topic	• Off-purpose

Holistic Scoring:

- **Variety:** A range of errors includes sentence formation, punctuation, capitalization, grammar usage, and spelling.

- **Severity:** Basic errors are more heavily weighted than higher-level errors.

- **Density:** The proportion of errors to the amount of writing done well. This includes the ratio of errors to the length of the piece.

TASK 3 LITERARY ANALYSIS

Page 143
1. b.

2. c.

3. c.

Page 144
4. a., b., g.

5. Prose Constructed-Response

Scoring Notes: Use the rubric to evaluate student responses. Responses may include but are not limited to:

- Kherdian writes poetry about things that affect him emotionally. Source #1 indicates that for Kherdian, the day his father participated in the softball game was a day that "stands out forever in my memory." Source #2 mentions how Kherdian was "deeply touched" by his father's action.

2	The response gives sufficient evidence of the ability to cite evidence to support arguments and/or ideas.
1	The response gives limited evidence of the ability to cite evidence to support arguments and/or ideas.
0	A response gets no credit if it provides no evidence of the ability to cite evidence to support arguments and/or ideas.

10-Point Literary Analysis Performance Task Writing Rubric (Grades 6–11)

Scoring Notes: This ten-point rubric is composed of three traits: Organization/Purpose, Evidence/Elaboration, and Conventions. Evaluate student responses using the criteria from each of the three traits and add the individual scores together to arrive at an overall score point value.

4-Point Literary Analysis Performance Task Writing Rubric (Grades 6–11)			
Score	**Organization/Purpose**		
4	The response has a clear and effective organizational structure, creating a sense of unity and completeness. The organization is fully sustained between and within paragraphs. The response is consistently and purposefully focused:		
	• controlling idea of a literary work(s) is clearly communicated, and the focus is strongly maintained for the purpose and audience	• consistent use of a variety of transitional strategies to clarify the relationships between and among ideas	• effective introduction and conclusion	• logical progression of ideas from beginning to end; strong connections between and among ideas with some syntactic variety
3	The response has an evident organizational structure and a sense of completeness. Though there may be minor flaws, they do not interfere with the overall coherence. The organization is adequately sustained between and within paragraphs. The response is generally focused:		
	• controlling idea of a literary work(s) is clear, and the focus is mostly maintained for the purpose and audience	• adequate use of transitional strategies with some variety to clarify the relationships between and among ideas	• adequate introduction and conclusion	• adequate progression of ideas from beginning to end; adequate connections between and among ideas

2	The response has an inconsistent organizational structure. Some flaws are evident, and some ideas may be loosely connected. The organization is somewhat sustained between and within paragraphs. The response may have a minor drift in focus:			
	• controlling idea of a literary work(s) may be somewhat unclear, or the focus may be insufficiently sustained for the purpose and/or audience	• inconsistent use of transitional strategies and/or little variety	• introduction or conclusion, if present, may be weak	• uneven progression of ideas from beginning to end; and/or formulaic; inconsistent or unclear connections between and among ideas
1	The response has little or no discernible organizational structure. The response may be related to the literary work(s) but may provide little or no focus:			
	• controlling idea may be confusing or ambiguous; response may be too brief or the focus may drift from the purpose and/or audience	• few or no transitional strategies are evident	• introduction and/or conclusion may be missing	• frequent extraneous ideas may be evident; ideas may be randomly ordered or have an unclear progression
NS	• Insufficient (includes copied text)	• In a language other than English	• Off-topic	• Off-purpose

	4-Point Literary Analysis Performance Task Writing Rubric (Grades 6–11)				
Score	**Evidence/Elaboration**				
4	The response provides thorough elaboration of the support/evidence for the thesis/controlling idea that includes the effective use of examples from the literary work(s). The response clearly and effectively develops ideas, using precise language:				
	• comprehensive evidence (examples and details) from the source material is integrated, relevant, and specific	• clear citations or attribution to source material	• effective use of a variety of elaborative techniques	• vocabulary is clearly appropriate for the audience and purpose	• effective, appropriate style enhances content
3	The response provides adequate elaboration of the support/evidence for the thesis/controlling idea that includes the use of examples from the literary work(s). The response adequately develops ideas, employing a mix of precise and more general language:				
	• adequate evidence (examples and details) from the source material is integrated and relevant, yet may be general	• adequate use of citations or attribution to source material	• adequate use of some elaborative techniques	• vocabulary is generally appropriate for the audience and purpose	• generally appropriate style is evident

2	The response provides uneven, cursory elaboration of the support/evidence for the thesis/controlling idea that includes uneven or limited use of examples from the literary work(s). The response develops ideas unevenly, using simplistic language:				
	• some evidence (examples and details) from the source material may be weakly integrated, imprecise, repetitive, vague, and/or copied	• weak use of citations or attribution to source material	• weak or uneven use of elaborative techniques; development may consist primarily of source summary	• vocabulary use is uneven or somewhat ineffective for the audience and purpose	• inconsistent or weak attempt to create appropriate style
1	The response provides minimal elaboration of the support/evidence for the thesis/controlling idea that includes little or no use of examples from the literary work(s). The response is vague, lacks clarity, or is confusing:				
	• evidence (examples and details) from the source material is minimal, irrelevant, absent, incorrectly used, or predominantly copied	• insufficient use of citations or attribution to source material	• minimal, if any, use of elaborative techniques	• vocabulary is limited or ineffective for the audience and purpose	• little or no evidence of appropriate style
NS	• Insufficient (includes copied text)	• In a language other than English	• Off-topic	• Off-purpose	

2-Point Literary Analysis Performance Task Writing Rubric (Grades 6–11)			
Score	**Conventions**		
2	The response demonstrates an adequate command of conventions:		
	• adequate use of correct sentence formation, punctuation, capitalization, grammar usage, and spelling		
1	The response demonstrates a partial command of conventions:		
	• limited use of correct sentence formation, punctuation, capitalization, grammar usage, and spelling		
0	The response demonstrates little or no command of conventions:		
	• infrequent use of correct sentence formation, punctuation, capitalization, grammar usage, and spelling		
NS	• Insufficient (includes copied text)	• In a language other than English	• Off-topic	• Off-purpose

Holistic Scoring:

- **Variety:** A range of errors includes sentence formation, punctuation, capitalization, grammar usage, and spelling.

- **Severity:** Basic errors are more heavily weighted than higher-level errors.

- **Density:** The proportion of errors to the amount of writing done well. This includes the ratio of errors to the length of the piece.